Where your money hides

Published by Apostle M. J. Mohlala
Cnr Lansdowne and Hammer Roads, Philippi, Cape Town 7750, South Africa
www.apostlemohlalaministries.co.za

First edition 2020

© Apostle M. J. Mohlala 2020

Project manager and editor: Joy Nel (Bushbaby Editorial Services)
Designer: Karen Lilje (Hybrid Creative)
Proofreader: Jennifer Leak
Printing by ABC Press, South Africa

ISBN 978-0-620-87514-1

Where your money hides

APOSTLE MUSAWENKOSI MOHLALA

The wise store up choice food and olive oil,
but fools gulp theirs down.

PROVERBS 21:20 [NEW INTERNATIONAL VERSION]

Contents

Acknowledgements

I WOULD LIKE to express my special gratitude, firstly and foremost, to The Almighty God for granting me the opportunity to write this book.

I would also like to express my deep and sincere gratitude to the following individuals for their dynamism, vision, sincerity and motivation that have deeply inspired me: Dr Thomas Baloyi, Dr MD Manyike, Dr Hope Peto and Bridget Cebisile Langa.

I am extremely grateful to my dearest mother Regina Mokoena, for her love, prayers and sacrifices in preparing me for my future.

I am very much thankful to my lovely children – Samukelisiwe, Karabo, Nondumiso, Lesedi and Azonika – for their love, understanding and prayers throughout my life's journey.

Also, I express my thanks to my siblings – Sbusiso Patrick, Nomfundo and Ndumiso – and my extended family, for their support and valuable prayers.

I will be forever grateful to The Shekainah Ministries and Apostle Mohlala Ministries family for their unwavering support to the calling I have for God's people.

Apostle Musawenkosi Mohlala: A prophetic voice of possibility

THE MISSION

It is not unusual on a feast Sunday for the tall, white structure which houses Apostle Mohlala Ministries to be heaving with up to 10 000 worshippers finding their place and space to be with God. It is amongst the largest congregations in Southern Africa.

It is also a church in which its eponymous pastor, Apostle Mohlala, likes to talk about the intersection of faith and belief – the evidence of things unseen that changes lives and turns things around – and to remind generations that what anyone really needs is God's love.

Apostle Mohlala, who presents a vigorous self-determination within a calm and pleasant demeanour, says: "I believe that making the impossible, possible, starts by receiving His love. That's faith.

"I encourage fighting for what you desire and I believe in doing it through God. Nothing great comes easy, but with God everything is possible. I have seen the word of God impact leaders to make a difference in the lives of South Africans and I've seen people changed by being better equipped to handle life."

THE CALLING

This path on life's journey started in the mid-1990s when Musawenkosi Mohlala was a young man growing up in kaNyamazane near Mbombela (Nelspruit) in Mpumalanga. It was then that he had his first vision.

"When I fell asleep, I would see myself preaching and speaking to a multitude of people, but I put it out of my mind. One night, I had a dream about an old man from my village. He said, 'Mohlala boy, I'm dying. Still you have not shown me the way.'

"Two days later I heard that the very same old man had died. These kinds of dreams continued until eventually the only thing I could do was to find out what I was being called to act upon."

After fasting for 40 days and 40 nights, Musa knew what he had to do.

Exactly three years later, Apostle Musawenkosi Mohlala was ordained and devoted himself to the ministry full time. But more change was to come. In

2001, while serving under Dr T.H. Baloyi, "the Lord spoke to me and told me to go to Cape Town".

"Not only was Cape Town far away, but I'd already outlined a plan for my future and to settle in Mpumalanga!"

Like Abraham, who had been instructed by God to *leave your country, your people and your father's household and go to the land I will show you* (Genesis 12:1), there was no turning back for Apostle Mohlala.

APOSTLE MOHLALA MINISTRIES

Since Apostle Mohlala's move to the Mother City, Apostle Mohlala Ministries has grown to become one of the largest congregations in Southern Africa, and has branches throughout South Africa, namely in the Western Cape, KwaZulu-Natal, Eastern Cape, Gauteng, North West and Mpumalanga. Today, Apostle Mohlala is one of the most recognisable and pivotal prophetic voices on the African continent, dedicated to fulfilling his mandate from God, which includes community outreaches and social responsibilities.

"I never just wanted a church with congregants. I wanted a family with sons and daughters, committed to freeing the oppressed and healing the sick. To lighten one's load means to walk freely and replenish the well-being of our communities."

It's a message that resonates nationally and internationally, and many people travel from all around Southern Africa to hear Apostle Mohlala's prophetic words.

APOSTLE MOHLALA, THE MAN

On his downtime, you may find Musa on the Somerset West Golf Club course, watching the news on television or reading. These mediums expand knowledge and perspective, both of which have impacted his preaching.

"But when I prepare for the weekly message, I like to be in a very quiet space. To be still, with God," says Apostle Mohlala.

"My favourite passage in Proverbs is Proverbs 1:7: *The fear of the Lord is the beginning of knowledge, but fools despise wisdom and instruction.* It's a message I carry with me always, even when it comes to finances. Jesus spoke about pointing to the need for good stewardship of the treasures that God gives us, along with the wisdom to do so.

"He will always meet our needs, if we let Him do so."

"Almost everyone wants to be wealthy, but only a few people truly know what they need to do in order to become wealthy. Knowing where your wealth is hidden is essential."

Introduction

HAVE YOU EVER wondered why you are not as wealthy as you once envisioned you would be? Have you tried all you can think of, yet you still have not managed to make a financial breakthrough? Have you taken up every opportunity that presented itself to you, but still find yourself unable to become as prosperous and rich as you intended to be?

Sometimes it is difficult and frustrating to see other people around you becoming wealthy rapidly while you do not. Ecclesiastes 10:19 says: *"A party gives laughter, wine gives happiness, and money gives everything!"* You need money in all aspects of your life.

Big goals require you to put in extra work and energy. Don't hold back your full potential. You must listen to your inner voice that says: "You can do it". Only you can convince yourself that it's possible and put your mind to it.

There are many stories about those who have failed because they listened to negative people and did not believe that they had the full potential to do great things and be successful. If you care about becoming successful in your life, rest assured that you will be successful. That's the first step, believing that you can succeed.

It's not enough to say you *want* something and then do not take the initiative to obtain it; you have to *do* something to achieve that goal. There are processes you have to go through before getting to the prize or the reward. Make these undertakings your one-way ticket to your dreams. Remember, people who succeed do not have the word "quit" in their vocabulary.

Thinking big is mandatory when you want to become rich. Learn to apply "zero-based thinking", a concept originated by Brian Tracy, a highly respected self-help author and motivational speaker. This concept simply allows you to evaluate yourself: if you are not happy with where you are currently, get moving, change what needs to be changed and start over.

Allow yourself to think and dream big. The late Steve Jobs, business magnate and co-founder of Apple Inc., once said:

"Life can be much broader once you discover one simple fact: Everything around you that you call life was made up by people that were no smarter than you and you can change it, you can influence it, and you can build your own things that other people can use.

Once you learn that, you'll never be the same again."

To get ahead, you need to adopt the entrepreneurial mindset of "I can create faster than anyone else can copy". There are other traits, too, that are common to people who are hungry for success, such as being a hard worker, honesty to earn respect, and how well you deal with situations and others.

Do not sit back and watch while others are making it big out there. Opportunities to become wealthy abound – empowering yourself with knowledge is an important step in taking up those opportunities.

There are places where your treasure is hidden and once you can identify these places, you can't go wrong. And that is what the aim is of this book – to teach you how to make money and accumulate wealth, how to multiply your wealth and, most importantly, to know where it's hiding and how to find it.

DECLARATION

*"I decree and I declare that you will never
be broke anymore in your life.*

*The money, the wealth that God has in you
must manifest now.*

You will have plenty.

*I decree from today you will never run out,
you will have more than enough.*

You will have abundantly above all you can expect.

You will have sufficiency in all things, always.

You will never lack according to the word of God.

From today you will not borrow but will lend out.

You will have more than enough resources.

I speak to money to come to you.

So shall it be; it can never be otherwise."

"Destiny can never be planned; it can only be discovered by trusting and following what feels right."

——— Find your destiny

AT DIFFERENT PHASES of our lives, we all find ourselves asking questions about our destiny. The most important questions we have to ask ourselves are:

- What is my destiny?
- How do I know when I have reached my destiny?
- Is what I'm doing with my life what I should be doing?

When a person cannot find purpose within themselves, they will search in vain if they try to find it elsewhere. Self-discovery is key!

The main goal you must have in mind is *reaching your destiny*. How you can achieve this? It is actually very simple. Destiny can never be planned; it can only be discovered by trusting and following what feels right.

Each one of us has a predestined purpose and physical place where God has foreordained for us to flourish. This could mean a change in your environment, job or company that can ultimately result in the fulfilment of your destiny. In order for you to achieve this, you have to seek God's guidance while pursuing your destiny.

There are places designated for success. The perfect example is Johannesburg in South Africa, also known as the City of Gold, or eGoli, because of its beginnings as a gold-mining town. The South African city built on gold. It is a city that is a destiny for many people and is said to be the modern-day hub of South African commerce.

1 Corinthians 10:23 [New International Version] says: *"I have the right to do anything,"* you say – but not everything is beneficial. "I have the right to do anything" – but not everything is constructive.

What this means is that you must choose to do what is beneficial to you and is worth taking up.

When God promises to give you land and wealth, you must obey and follow His instructions. He always delivers on his promises. This is illustrated in the following extract:

Joshua sends spies to Jericho
Joshua 2:2, 8–13

² From Shittim, Joshua, son of Nun, secretly sent out two men as spies. He told them, "Go, look at that country, especially the city of Jericho." So they went to Jericho and entered the house of a prostitute named Rahab to spend the night there.

⁸ Before the spies fell asleep, Rahab went up to them on the roof. ⁹ She said to them, "I know the Lord will give you this land. Your presence terrifies us. All the people in this country are deathly afraid of you. ¹⁰ We've heard how the Lord dried up the water of the Red Sea in front of you when you left Egypt. We've also heard what you did to Sihon and Og, the two kings of the Amorites, who ruled east of the Jordan River. We've heard how you destroyed them for the Lord. [11] When we heard about it, we lost heart. There was no courage left in any of us because of you. The Lord your God is the God of heaven and earth. [12] Please swear by the Lord that you'll be as kind to my father's family as I've been to you. Also give me some proof [13] that you'll protect my father, mother, brothers, sisters, and their households, and that you'll save us from death."

DECLARATION

*"I decree and I declare that whatsoever was done in the
Spiritual realm to manipulate your destiny be reversed.*

*I refuse for you to go through what
your parents went through.*

Poverty is not your portion.

*I decree and I declare that your future
is ordained, predestined by God.*

You are the work of the hands of God.

*Take your things by force, your career by force,
your money by force,*

your house in the name of Jesus Christ.

You are not going to fail in your life.

You are going to make it to your destiny.

May God simplify and interpret your dreams.

So shall it be; it can never be otherwise."

"... before you can
become great,
you must discover
your greatness."

Discover who you are

GOD IS ALMIGHTY and omniscient – he knows every-thing. He has given us the ability to be great. But before you can become great, you must discover your great-ness. It is your mandate. You discover who you are from who you are not.

Not every bad thing is bad. Take, for example, the story of Wallace Johnson, builder of numerous Holiday Inn motels and convalescent hospitals:

> *"When I was forty years old. I worked in a sawmill. One morning the boss told me: 'You're fired!' Depressed and discouraged, I felt like the world had caved in on me.*
>
> *"It was during the Depression, and my wife and I greatly needed the small wages I had been earning. When I went home, I told my wife what had happened. She asked, 'What are you going to do now?'*
>
> *"I replied, 'I'm going to mortgage our little home, and go into the building business.'*

"My first venture was the construction of two small build-ings. Within five years, I was a multi-millionaire!

"Today, if I could locate the man who fired me, I would sincerely thank him for what he did. At the time it happened, I didn't understand why I was fired. Later, I saw that it was God's unerring and wondrous plan to get me into the way of His choosing!"

Your greatest enemy is not looking beyond your current achievements. If you are too comfortable with where you are right now, you won't gain much going forward. Leave your comfort zone and aim even higher.

When we read through the Gospels, we find many miracles that have obvious correlations with the rest of Jesus's ministry. For example, The Bible records that Jesus performed miracles with fish several times. In all but one instance, the fish were to feed the people, not to enrich them. However, in one miracle He told His disciples to go and catch a specific fish, then open its mouth and there would be money inside.

What these miracles illustrate is that not every fish has money in it. There is a specific fish for your destiny – you will be able to find your fish once you discover your destiny. Even gold is not everywhere – it is found in specific places. Find a specific place where you will become great.

Set a timeline for yourself: In so many years I want to see myself [where] and having achieved [what].

Sometimes, in life, people don't succeed because they haven't discovered/shifted their place of destiny.

Discovery – The Story of Moses

Moses' life is divided into three major sections of 40 years each. The first 40 years were spent in Pharaoh's court; the second 40 in the desert of Midian; and the last 40 in the desert of Sinai.

It is the natural tendency of humanity to desire privilege and pleasure, but Moses refused both of these. In human perspectives, Moses was guaranteed a life of privilege and pleasure if he had wanted it to be so. The Pharaoh's daughter had raised him as her own after she found him by the river. As an offspring of the palace, Moses had access to the very best of everything, and he became skilful in all that was provided for him. Moses was educated in all the wisdom of the Egyptians and was powerful in speech and action. (Acts 7:22).

Moses was a gifted leader who God used to bring about His plan for Israel and the world.

First, Moses rejected his royal position: By faith Moses, when he became of age [40 years old, Acts 7:23], refused to be called the son of Pharaoh's daughter. (*Hebrews 11:24). This decision was an act of faith. He chose to leave his royal privilege in Egypt and identify with the Israelite slaves (Exodus 1:8–14).*

What did Moses believe that made this choice possible? He believed that God would reward his choice; he believed that God was all-knowing; He believed that with God nothing was impossible. We should be like Moses and discover ourselves.

Prince Serge Wolkonsky, an influential Russian theatrical worker, once declared [in 1893] that "Business is the alpha and omega of American life. There is no pleasure, no joy, no satisfaction. There is no standard except that of profit. There is no other country where they speak of a man as worth so many dollars ... here they exist for business."

If you want to achieve greatness and financial wealth, you need to find a healthy balance between making money and enjoying the other important things in life, such as family, hobbies and leisure time.

DECLARATION

"I decree and I declare that you will find favour

*From the people God has assigned
to take you to your destiny;*

*They will come from the West, East,
North and South to find you.*

This is your season to succeed.

*I see people coming your way bringing silver,
gold, opportunities, success and connections.*

*Coming to connect you with what
you have been praying about.*

They are coming from all angles.

So shall it be; it can never be otherwise."

Heavenly Father, help me to distinguish whenever the offer of human privilege is competing with Your will for my life. Help me to discover my destiny and trust Your ways. Open my eyes so that I can identify my place of destiny. Amen.

DECLARATION

*"I decree and I declare that this is your time and
season for the resurrection of your financial affairs.*

You will never go down anymore.

*I remove your name from the list
of people who are going down.*

You are going up.

This season shall end with joy, success and celebration.

Receive Grace to another level.

*May God lift you. You are next in line
for your testimony.*

No more suffering, no more poverty.

I declare that your ways are opening.

So shall it be; it can never be otherwise."

"Attract all kinds
of material
and financial
abundance into
your life."

Dimensions of wealth

A PERSON HAS to make it a norm to attract and manifest all kinds of material and financial abundance into their life. It's helpful to break down the different dimensions of wealth, which can be grouped into different categories that can impact your financial decisions. This will help you move towards discovering your treasure, wealth and success. As you embark on a journey of no return into your financial success, take note of the following:

Financial wealth is the net worth, assets and liabilities of a person.

Spiritual/Ethical wealth is guided by principles, ethics, values and any spiritual beliefs that help direct one's vision in life.

Experiential wealth refers to the experiences, such as travels, hobbies, career, and so on, that have shaped a person into who they are.

Relational wealth refers to connections that one has built with people, be it friends, family or colleagues.

When your life and financial situation change and you are getting more than you are used to, you'll need to modify your situation and be in line with the progression. But to successfully navigate a new financial reality, you have to familiarise yourself with the following terms, and align your expertise accordingly.

Transitional wealth is the value you provide, i.e. when you exchange a service for reward. Transitional change is a change made to replace existing processes with new processes, but having the same strategy in mind.

Transformational wealth is the influence you create in life. Transformational change is a change made to completely alter the structure of something, not just the processes.

Sovereign wealth is wealth from the finger of God, also known as a Mystery of Divine Supply. This is mentioned in The Bible in 1 Kings 17 [New International Version], when God promised Elijah that he will supply him with food and drink while he was in the Kerith Ravine, east of the Jordan.

> [4] *You will drink from the brook,*
> *and I have ordered the ravens to feed you there.*
> [6] *The ravens brought him bread and meat*
> *in the morning and bread and meat in the evening, and*
> *he drank from the brook.* 1 Kings 17: 4; 6

DECLARATION

"I decree and I declare that it is not too late for you to

Accomplish everything God has placed in your heart.

You have not missed your window of opportunity.

God is releasing a special Grace to help you
accomplish your dreams.

This is your time, this is your moment. Receive it today.

In Jesus' name.

So shall it be; it can never be otherwise."

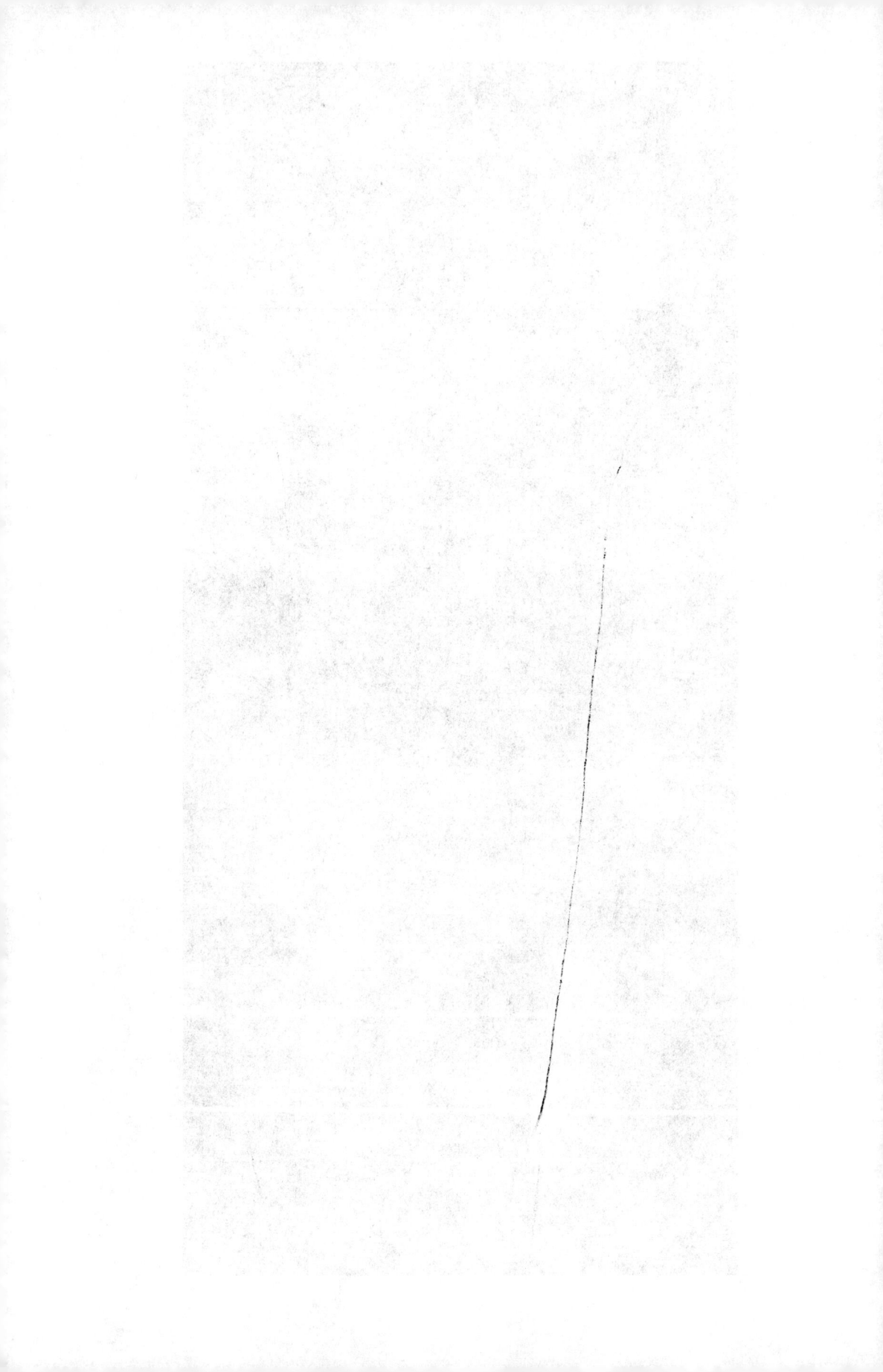

"The money you want
is already waiting
in someone's bank
account. What do
you have to exchange
for that money?"

Your money hides in people

PEOPLE ARE MONEY. This includes the people you live with, people you meet throughout your lifetime and even people that you do not know and will never meet.

If people are money, you can strategise about how you can access the money from people. Use the same principles and techniques that you apply to other tasks to plan how you can attract money from others. Let them pay you so that you can acquire your wealth.

Remember this: You don't have to pay anything to think, but you can get paid to think correctly.

Be creative in your own way. In the words of billionaire Sheldon Adelson: "If you do things differently, success will follow you like your shadow. And you can't get rid of it!" Dare to be unique and that will make you stand out.

You can attract money easily. But in order for you to be able to realise that people are money, you must have something valuable to exchange for that money.

Create the need so that you can always be needed by people to fulfil their needs and they pay you in return for taking care of their needs.

For example, pioneering scientists, programmers and engineers saw a need for an "information super-highway" and they each developed new features and technologies that eventually merged to become the Internet. And in another example, even though we are born with hair, someone saw the need to create weaves and now there are many people who make money out of that need.

You must recognise that the money you need is with people. The car that you want is parked in someone's garage or at a car dealership. The house you want, someone is staying in it. You must have a way and a proper strategy in place in order for you to acquire what you want.

One of the strategies you need in order for you to acquire what you want is to place a value on yourself. People only give money and invest it where they see value. If there is no value, money cannot be attracted.

To give an example of how value is placed on someone, consider the African custom of *ilobolo* (dowry) negotiations, in which the bride's family places a value on their daughter. The higher the price, the more valuable she is to them. Even if the negotiators complain that the price is too high (and the daughter, too, may plead with her parents to bring the dowry down), the value has been indicated and that is what must be paid. When agreeing to the *ilobolo*, the groom is also indicating the value of the bride.

So, in essence, when you place a value on yourself, that is what people must pay. And if they pay, then they accept that that is your value.

Money flows in the direction of value. *Where there is no value, there is no money.* In other words, if you under-value yourself, others will do so too.

If you observe people who are successful and wealthy, you will notice that they do not give away money without receiving something of value in return. They *exchange* money for value. For example, even when the wealthy donate money to charity, they often do so as a means to gain positive publicity for their business, which encourages the public to support their business and increases revenue.

This is why it is vital to place a value on yourself. Create your value, make it known to people and money shall come to you.

KNOW YOUR VALUE AND YOUR WORTH

At times we overlook our amazing abilities because we are distracted by our weaknesses. It is important to accept and be content with our weaknesses and eccentricities. Acknowledging your uniqueness and discovering how you can contribute to the world with your gifts is a profound and life-changing experience. It is also important to ask yourself *how* you can use your exceptional life story to help others.

When you are determining your value, there are certain things you must bear in mind. Take, for instance, someone who specialises in painting walls. In the beginning they may take a full day to paint one room and charge you three thousand rand. As they gain more experience and get better at painting houses, it may take only two hours to complete one room, yet they will still charge you three thousand rand. Why, you may ask, do they charge the same amount for completing the same job in a fraction of the time?

The answer is this: you should be compensated for your *value* rather than the time it takes to achieve a given task.

KNOW HOW TO CALCULATE YOUR WORTH

Put a price on 'it'. It is very important that you know exactly what you are worth. First and foremost, your true cost is based on what you honestly believe you could earn on your own, using your existing gifts, talents, strengths and skills to solve problems for others. For example, if you are good at cooking, you can use your skill to cook for people and charge them for your services.

Here are some tips to help you get on the right track:

Know your metrics

It is very important that you track your metrics in order for you to succeed. But, what are metrics? In basic terms, when referring to business, metrics are a set of statistics or figures that measure results, and these can vary from one type of business to another.

Tracking metrics makes it easier to run your business, as this assists and guides you into knowing where to invest your resources, and helps you focus on the most critical issues. Tracking metrics also improves the performance and outcome of your business. By tracking metrics you can quickly identify any problems in your business.

If you want to focus and be known for providing the best service in your chosen field, then you must track multiple customer service metrics such as response times, returns, and customer satisfaction surveys. We've all heard the phrase "you can't improve what you can't measure". If you aren't tracking a metric, how do you know if you're improving? Knowing and measuring your metrics makes it much easier for you to grow a more successful business.

Know your market value

Knowing what you're worth is essential. Knowing your market value is key to getting the pay you deserve for the services you provide. Estimating your market value is both an art and a science. Start by estimating the market value for your skillset and experience in your chosen field.

Know what's within your control.
Aim high and do everything in your control to become your best self and excel in what you do and the projects you undertake.

See opportunities and take risks where others see difficulties. This way you will be able to do what others could not do before you.

Money, I call on you to know my name. I decree and I declare that I shall suffer no more. Money will locate me. There is money with my name written on it. And no one shall touch it until it reaches me. Everything that belongs to me, shall come to me. Those who owe me money, they shall bring it back. So shall it be; it can never be otherwise. In the name of Jesus Christ, I call money to come to me. Amen.

DECLARATION

*"I decree and I declare that God's abundance
is surrounding your life today.*

*I declare that breakthroughs are coming into your life,
sudden bursts of God's goodness.*

So shall it be; it can never be otherwise."

"In order for you to make the money you want, you must ask God for the wisdom to be able to identify problems to which you can provide the solutions. In this way, you will start making money."

—— Your money hides in people's problems

IF YOU WANT money from people, you must be able to solve their problems. Where there are problems, there is money.

Every problem, no matter how large or small, holds a hidden financial treasure in its solution.

What is a problem for one person is a treasure for someone else. This is why you should pray to God to give you wisdom to identify people's problems and the know-how to solve them and, in so doing, to make money flow in your direction.

Work smart, not hard. This concept holds true when you know how to apply it. Problems are there to be solved. The mistake we make is that we sit and discuss the problems instead of creating a solution for them. When someone comes to you with a problem, be smart and quick enough to have a solution for it. This is another way of attracting money, as you can charge them for solving those problems.

Every day, people or companies make money by solving problems. For example, on a most basic level, companies such as Coca-Cola and KFC provide a solution to thirst and hunger by manufacturing soft drinks and tasty fried chicken that also satisfy our addiction to junk food. On a more significant level, medical doctors make money by solving problems associated with various illnesses, while therapists sit and listen to people talk about their problems and earn money for providing this service.

There are so many people with problems and they are looking to pay others to solve those problems. It is up to you to identify these people and come up with the solution they need. And if those people happen to be wealthy and you are able to solve their problems, then you in turn will attract wealth.

While some people may believe that money can be found by sitting behind a desk in a fancy corporate office, I will tell you that this is not really the case. Rather, money is hidden in the problems that are solved by the people sitting behind these desks. More importantly, you can make money by solving people's problems no matter where you are.

Did you know that a number of the richest people in the world are not highly educated? Some are even high school dropouts. I most definitely am not saying that education is unimportant. Quite the opposite, in fact, as it is very important in this day and age. But when it comes to making money, these "uneducated" people created their immense wealth by identifying the problems that needed solutions and they came up with strategies and a plan to solve them. That is how money came flowing to them.

Don't see a problem and complain; see a problem and pray for wisdom on how you can solve it and charge for those services. That will, without doubt, make money flow in your direction.

Oh God, create a problem for someone who has money, and give me the wisdom and knowledge I need so that I can solve it. Amen.

DECLARATION

*"I decree and I declare that you will put
actions behind your faith.*

You will not be passive or indifferent.

*You will take bold steps to move towards your success
and God will show up and do amazing things.*

So shall it be; it can never be otherwise."

PROBLEM VS SOLUTION

Here are a few everyday examples of how people have identified problems and how they provide the solutions. Use this list as inspiration to do the same.

PROBLEM	SOLUTION
You are ill.	A doctor will help to make you well again.
You are getting divorced or have been arrested.	A lawyer will help to conclude the divorce or to get you out of jail.
You need a place to stay.	A real estate agent or property broker will help you buy a house or rent an apartment.
You have an important function to go to and need to look your best.	A hair stylist can help to style your hair, a makeup artist can make you look great, and a fashion retailer can sell you the clothes you need for the occasion.
You are struggling with your schoolwork or university course.	A tutor can help improve your understanding of the subject(s) and bump up your marks.

PROBLEM	SOLUTION
You have a leaking pipe or problems with your electrical wiring.	A plumber or an electrician can fix the problem.
You don't have the time to make your garden look good.	A gardener or garden service company can do the work for you.
You want to have fun at a party, but don't want to drink and drive.	A taxi or professional driving service can drive you home.
You work long hours and don't have the time to take the dog to the parlour or for a walk.	A dog-grooming service can groom your dog and a dog-walking service can help to keep your pet fit and healthy.
Your daughter is getting married and you want her to have the wedding of her dreams.	An event coordinator can plan and execute the entire wedding according to your budget.
You are renovating your home and need to store some of your bigger household items while the work is completed.	A temporary and secure storage facility can be used to keep the items safe until you need them again.

DECLARATION

"I decree and I declare that you are equipped
for every good work God has planned for you.

Every bondage, every limitation is
being broken off you.

This is your time to shine.

You will rise higher, overcome every obstacle,
and experience victory like never before.

So shall it be; it can never be otherwise."

"A gift opens the way and ushers the giver into the presence of the great."

PROVERBS 18:16
[NEW INTERNATIONAL VERSION]

Your money hides in your gifts and talents

EVERYONE HAS A God-given gift. When we are born, we come out with our hands folded and it is believed that this symbolises holding onto the gifts you have been given. So, when a person says that they have no talent, tell them that is untrue. They just need to dig deeper to find it.

We all have gifts and talents. The Bible, in Proverbs 18:16, says that your gift shall usher you into the presence of the great.

Your gift shall make room for you.

Can you run?

Can you jump?

Can you sing?

Can you cook?

Can you talk?

Can you cry?

Can you laugh?

If you can do any of the above or more, then you can make money from what you do best.

Do not undermine your gift. Develop it so that it can usher you into greatness and bring you wealth. When you understand what you are born with, you will never go poor.

Take, for example, the South African music artist known as Mandoza. He may not have had the greatest voice, but he had a gift and he used it to make it in the music industry. What this means is that your money is hidden in your gift. Once you discover your gift, you have discovered your destiny.

We must put more effort into developing our gifts and talents. The United States of America is powerful and wealthy because it puts in effort to develop people's gifts, so much so that they are celebrated across the globe.

Some people have what is known as "the gift of the gab", or the ability to speak articulately and persuasively. Motivational speakers are one such example. But there are many other gifts, such as dancing, singing or running. Whatever gift you have, nurture it and make money using it.

Some people do not realise how powerful they truly are because they do not know what gifts they are carrying and have not yet been discovered. If you use your talents wisely, you will defeat poverty.

RECOGNISE YOUR TALENTS AND USE THEM TO ACCUMULATE WEALTH

The easiest way to build wealth is by making full use of your talents.

Recognising your natural talents can be quite difficult. In order to do so, there are questions you have to ask yourself.

The first one is: What excited or stimulated me most as a child?

Recall your happiest memories. For example, would you be impatient for the school day to end so that you could go and play volley ball on the beach, or go and swim with your friends in a muddy river or dam, or even to sit quietly and draw or build things at home? Would you get so caught up in what you were doing that you'd sometimes lose track of time and get into trouble with your parents for coming home so late?

It is likely that the same things you loved to do as a child are still the things that motivate you today. The only difference is that now you use that talent in a different environment. To utilise your talent and make money from it, you need to find a way to align the work you do today with what made you happy in the past.

Another question you must ask yourself is: What are the things that make me lose track of time?

These are the things on which you focus fully, sometimes even to the point of going without sleep once you start undertaking them.

These are your talents, and they should be nurtured and developed. Do not stifle or suppress them.

Know your strengths and weaknesses
Knowing what your personal strengths are is also key to allocating your money. Your biggest personal strength would be something that comes very easily for you; it comes naturally. You can look at the attributes that represent you the most, for example, you don't have difficulty speaking to a stranger or you are artistic, entertaining. It could be anything.

It is equally important to know your weaknesses as much as knowing your strengths. Your weaknesses hold you back from achieving many great things. You have the power to work on and improve these weaknesses, be they anything from professional to social skills.

- Place value on your assignment.
- Know your opponent.
- Know your potential and understand your strength.
- Have a role model in life.
- If the vision you have is not bigger than you, then God is not in it.
- You cease to be ordinary.
- You are meant to command money in unconventional ways.

Market yourself

Put yourself out there, and start becoming known for the services you offer. Identify opportunities and platforms to formally and informally share your expertise and thoughts.

Most importantly, you must learn to have fun while doing what you are good at. If you are happy with what you are doing, the results will be outstanding. You must be looking forward to waking up to do the job.

May my gift be unleashed. May my gift be released. May I discover my gift and appreciate it. May I use my gift wisely so that I can attract money. So shall it be; it can never be otherwise. Amen.

DECLARATION

*"I decree and I declare that unexpected
blessings are coming your way.*

*You will move forward from barely making
it to having more than enough.*

God will open up supernatural doors for you.

So shall it be; it can never be otherwise."

"If we knew then what we know now, we would be a lot further in life. Knowledge is key."

Your money hides in information

KNOWLEDGE IS POWER and you are as powerful as what you know.

Fortunately, information is an unlimited resource and there is therefore no limit to how powerful you can become.

In order to grow, you need to accumulate information to expand your knowledge. However, you cannot expand your knowledge beyond the information you currently have, so it is vital that you continue accumulating information at every opportunity.

There are many ways to accumulate information, from structured education (for example, school or university) and staying up-to-date on what's happening around the world by following the news, to travelling to different countries and being exposed to diverse cultures and experiences.

Ignorance can be very costly. It allows people to take advantage of you. To make it in life, you need to be armed with the knowledge of what is happening around you so that you know where you stand. Knowledge provides the key to recognising where the opportunities are to make money.

Improve yourself on a daily basis. That will also help you get new ideas.

PRAYER

Dear God, truly you are a God of abundance. May you direct and guide me as I accumulate information and grow and advance into new levels of prosperity. Amen.

DECLARATION

*"I decree and I declare that whatever
you put your hands to will prosper and succeed.*

You will experience a new sense of freedom.

*In the spiritual realm things have been set
into motion and blessings are on their way to you.*

So shall it be; it can never be otherwise."

"Seek wealth, not money or status. Wealth is having assets that earn while you sleep. Money is how we transfer time and wealth. Status is your place in the social hierarchy."

NAVAL RAVIKANT

Money flows in a direction of value

I DON'T BELIEVE that luck leads to success. Luck is defined as success or failure brought on by chance, whereas I believe it is brought about by your own abilities or efforts. Roman philosopher Seneca's words, "Luck is when preparation meets opportunity", reminds us that we create our own luck.

The value you place on your gifts and talents will attract people. Everyone has money, but they won't give it to you until you have something of value that they need. If you have something that is in demand, you can use it to create value, and by letting people know that you have it, money will come to you.

To establish long-term relationships and long-time success with your clients, you must create value for them as well. Establish a relationship that is built on honesty. That will build trust between you and them. It's a mutual benefit.

Some people make money from scamming and manipulating people, but this only works for a short period of time and it often has very bad consequences. Honesty is crucial.

I decree and I declare that from today onwards, I will have something of value, something that is in demand, which will attract money to come my way.
Amen.

DECLARATION

"I decree and I declare the protection of God over you.

Your needs shall be met.

I bring you before God; your progress shall be easy.

You shall stand out.

I command supernatural rain over you.

May the earth favour you.

I command every barren ground to become fruitful.

You will obtain favour before God and men.

So shall it be; it can never be otherwise."

"Then the Lord replied: Write down the revelation and make it plain on tablets so that a herald may run with it."

HABAKKUK 2:2
[NEW INTERNATIONAL VERSION]

—— Money hides in your vision

Vision commences with dreaming. A genuine dream is about existing for something that's bigger than you. It's your life's resolution, your assignment, the reason you were created and how you are going to change the world. The kind of legacy you will leave behind. It's the impact you want to make in the lives of others.

> *"Vision is the art of seeing things invisible."*
> – Jonathan Swift

Having visions is familiar to many of us, but most people do not take the time to do visioning. Clarifying your vision is one of the most powerful techniques to bring instantaneous change to your life. If you have personal vision, do you have one for your business?

It is essential that your business goals and your personal goals are aligned. When you live by your vision, everything changes. That is another aspect of where your money hides.

Write a mission statement and list the steps you need to take to achieve your vision.

These are the tools and steps to guide you when writing your vision.

- Find a comfortable place to write your vision.
- Use your imagination.
- Ask yourself personal questions.
- Remember, a big part of this is spiritual.
- Create a dream inventory.

Your vision must be:

- Ideal
- Unique
- Tangible
- Future-oriented
- For the common good

Bind yourself to your vision

Surround yourself with people who will help you stay the course and who will encourage and challenge you to achieve your vision.

Make room for change

Accept that you may need to adjust or alter your vision every so often as circumstances and time dictate. See your vision as a living thing.

You have been created with a purpose and exceptional gifts to share with the people around you.

When your vision is clearly stated and you understand it, plan how you are going to make money from it.

Let my vision be
clear to me. Let me
be given wisdom to
discover my vision.
May I prosper and
never go weary
as I embark on
this journey of
accumulating
my wealth.
Amen.

DECLARATION

*"I decree and I declare that every wicked
power that has targeted your finances
be nullified, and may it die by fire.*

I declare a breakthrough for you.

May God set a crown of gold over your head.

So shall it be; it can never be otherwise."

"Money is a tool. Used properly it makes something beautiful; used wrong, it makes a mess!"

BRADLEY VINSON

Money hides in goods and services/products

THERE IS A SECRET in buying and selling goods for profit.

Some people use the global marketplace to make a lot of money. It is important to discover an easy money-making method and how to make it work for you. With a little shopping practicality, you can turn the global marketplace into your own personal moneymaking mechanism.

USING MONEY TO MAKE MONEY: ARBITRAGE

The old secret has it that to get rich is very simple: buy at a low price and sell at a high price. So an alternative use of your money would be to buy goods not to consume, but to resell. This process is known as arbitrage.

DECLARATION

*"I decree and I declare that the spirit of
fear be broken over your life.*

*The spirit of struggle,
The spirit of shame, disgrace, dishonour, poverty,*

let it be broken.

In Jesus' name.

So shall it be; it can never be otherwise."

Where your money hides

1. Money hides in people

2. Money hides in people's problems

3. Money hides in opportunities

4. Money hides in gifts and talents

5. Money hides in ideas

6. Money hides in goods and services/products

DECLARATION

"I decree and I declare that you will be promoted.

You will be exalted.

I declare that you will be celebrated.

I declare that you will prosper.

Whatever your hands have started,
Your hands will finish it.

So shall it be; it can never be otherwise."

Dear God, anoint
my eyes to see the
hidden riches of
this world. May I
receive the power
and anointing to
gain wealth in Jesus'
name. I know and I
believe that it is done
in the name of Jesus.
Amen.

DECLARATION

"I decree and I declare that Jehovah will grant you speed.

Every evil power mandated to destroy your destiny,

May it die by fire.

So shall it be; it can never be otherwise."

www.ingramcontent.com/pod-product-compliance
Lightning Source LLC
Chambersburg PA
CBHW051337200326
41519CB00026B/7460